Breakup Survival Manual (And How Not to Get Back with Your Ex)

Alina A. Rubi

Published independently.

Author: Alina A. Rubi

Email: rubiediciones29@gmail.com

Editing: Angeline Rubi

Editorial contact: rubiediciones29@gmail.com

The Beginning of the End (and the Beginning of Something New)

No one wakes up on a Monday morning thinking they're going to lose the love of their life between unanswered WhatsApp messages, a list of sad songs, and a cup of warm coffee. But here you are, reading these lines with a little broken heart, eyes a little swollen and soul trying to convince the brain that it is not worth writing again to that person who has already made it clear that they do not want to be. Or worse, that he does not know how to be.

Love breakups don't come with instructions, although they should. You don't train for this like you train for a marathon. There is no warm-up, there is no stopwatch, there is no medal. There is only silence, anxiety, obsessive thoughts and a little inner voice that repeats: "What if it was all my fault?" Surprise: it wasn't, at least not everything.

This book is born from that wound that we all carry with dissimulation, that emptiness that we leave in bed when someone leaves, and that emotional whirlwind that comes uninvited when things don't go as we expected. But it is also born from the certainty that no one dies of love, although sometimes it seems that we are one step away from the drama soap opera with tears included.

Here you will not find cheesy self-help phrases or rituals to attract your ex with scented candles and a full moon. This is not a manual for getting anyone back but you. It is a practical guide, brutally honest and with the touch of sarcasm necessary to laugh between tears.

We are going to talk about everything that hurts, what confuses, what burns and what is difficult to let go of. But we're also going to laugh a little about our own mental soap operas, about the times we watched like detectives with mastery in digital espionage, and about that glorious moment when we finally blocked those who should be left out.

Because yes, the heart can break, but it can also be rebuilt with new bricks, better choices and zero want to beg for affection. And if there's one good thing about a breakup, it's that it can be the push you need to come back to you, with more strength, more clarity, and a lot less drama.

Welcome to your rebirth. Here begins the journey back home: you.

Recognize the pain and difficulty of the moment

Accepting that it hurts is the first step, although sometimes we would like to skip straight to the part where everything is already fine, and we laugh about what happened while drinking wine with friends saying "thank goodness it left". But no, before the toast comes the fall. And denying it only hurts more. You're not exaggerating, you're not being weak, you're not dramatizing. You are going through a real loss, even if there is no coffin or flowers, even if no one gives you condolences.

The heart does not understand logic, or well-intentioned advice such as "someone better will appear". What he understands is that someone who was part of your day-to-day life is no longer there, that routines were broken, that future plans were left floating in the air like balloons without an owner. And that hurts. Because love is invested with body, time, dreams and trust. And when it is broken, not only is the bond broken, but also parts of you that you had given without asking for a receipt are broken.

There are days when getting out of bed is already a feat. Moments when silence weighs more than an argument. You're not crazy if you hear his voice in your head, if you inertia check his networks, if you feel like calling him just to find out if it hurts, even a little bit. You have to recognize that you are in that place, in that uncomfortable hole, that is what begins to move the air. Because what is named is transformed.

It is not easy. Not fast either. But you're here, feeling, even if you don't like what you feel. And that, although it may not seem like it, is a form of resistance. Because those who feel, live. And those who dare to feel it even when it burns... They end up stronger than ever. So yes: you're in the middle of chaos. And that, believe it or not, is a good sign. Because from chaos the most powerful rebirths are born.

Warning: The path is not easy, but it is possible and worth it

Let's be clear from the beginning: this is not a magic recipe, nor a foolproof spell to erase your ex from memory as if it were emotional spam. There are no shortcuts or inspirational phrases that cut the void from one day to the next. What there is a process. Long, ugly at times, uncomfortable almost always... but absolutely necessary.

You're going to stumble. With songs, with memories, with places, with old messages that you didn't have the courage to erase. You're going to have emotional relapses, "maybe it wasn't that bad" days, and "what if I write to you just to check on your dog?" Take it easy. That's all part of the journey. This path is not straight, nor clean, nor Instagram-friendly. But it's yours.

There will be times when you want to give up. Return. To the known evil. To the lukewarm. To which it did not give you peace, but at least it was familiar to you. And right there, on that emotional curve, is when you're going to need to remind yourself the most why you came out. Because you're worth it. Because you deserve more. Because loving shouldn't hurt every day.

Yes, I tell you with brutal sincerity: you are going to cry. But you're also going to laugh, and you're going to discover parts of yourself that you didn't even know were asleep. You're going to build a new version of yourself that no longer settles for emotional crumbs or kneels for attention.

So, if at any point you feel like you're going backwards, remember this: healing is not a straight line. It's a clumsy dance. And every step, even the one you think is going backwards, is teaching you something. It is not easy. But believe me when I tell you: it's possible. And, above all, it is worth it. Because at the end of the road there is not your ex. There is you. More alive, stronger and much freer.

Accepting Reality: The First Step to Healing

Denial and shock: Why does it hurt so much?

When a relationship ends, the first instinct of the heart is to say: "This is not happening". Your head knows it, the ignored messages confirm it, even your friends have already told you that it is not convenient for you. But there is a part of you that resists, as if it were convinced that it is all a cosmic misunderstanding and that at any moment that person is going to knock on the door with a repentant face and a bouquet of cheap flowers.

Denial is not cowardice, it is self-protection. It is the soul's mode of emergence when something breaks, and it still does not know how to stand on its own. And although it may seem useless, that denial is also part of the process. The problem is to stay there for too long, justifying the unjustifiable, idealizing what hurt and denying what was obvious.

Shock, on the other hand, is that emptiness that leaves you staring at the ceiling without knowing what day it is or why the body weighs so much. It is the state of alertness of the heart that does not understand why someone who claimed to love you now does not answer even a "hello". It is as if the soul has collided head-on with a wall and the body is still on autopilot.

And it hurts. Of course it hurts. Not because you're weak, but because you gambled. Because you gave time, dreams, tenderness. Because you projected a future and that future has just imploded in front of your eyes. What hurts the most is not always the absence of the person, but the fall of everything you imagined with them.

Accepting reality doesn't mean at once stopping crying or running out to do yoga and affirmations in front of the mirror. To accept is to look at yourself without filters and say: "Yes, it's over. He is not coming back. And even if it hurts, I'm going to continue." It is to stop waiting for messages that do not arrive, happy endings that do not exist and signs that are only excuses disguised as hope.

Accepting is not giving up. It is to regain power. Because when you stop fighting with what was, you start building what can be. Even if you don't know how yet. Even if at first you walk trembling. The first step is not taken with certainty. It is given with courage. And you got it. Even if you don't see it today.

Allowing yourself to feel: Validating emotions (sadness, anger, fear, confusion)

In a world where everyone seems to be in a hurry to "get over it," stopping to cry can feel like a weakness. But it is not. It's a sign that you're alive. And more importantly: it is a sign that you are healing, even if it seems otherwise. Allowing oneself to feel is not sinking into drama, it is daring to cross the emotional bridge without anesthesia. It's giving space to what hurts, so it doesn't get trapped in the body disguised as insomnia, anxiety, or misdirected anger.

Sadness comes like a tide: silent, constant, and unstoppable. And that's okay. You're not failing because you miss, cry, or it hurts to breathe. You're grieving. You're saying goodbye to a part of your life. Don't minimize it. What you felt was real, even if the other person left as if nothing had happened.

Then comes the anger. The one that burns inside and sometimes disguises itself as sarcasm or the desire to break the cell phone. You are angry because you gave more than you received, because you kept quiet about what hurt, because you waited for gestures that never came. You don't have to justify your anger or suppress it with phrases such as "you have to be mature". Being mature is also knowing when to say "so far" with eyes full of fire.

Fear appears in the form of questions: what if no one loves me again? what if they fail me again? what if I never get over it? Answer this: fear is part of the package. It's normal to fear the unknown, especially when the familiar was your usual zone. But if the love you have hurt you, the unknown isn't so scary. It gives me hope.

And then there's the confusion. That mental cloud where you wonder if you did it right, if it was your fault, if you could have done something more. The answer is no. You did what you knew how to do with the tools you had. And if you're confused now, it's because you're rearranging everything inside. The pieces of the puzzle don't fit together right away. Give it time.

Feeling doesn't make you weak. To repress yourself yes. This is not the time to be strong by force, nor to smile when you can't handle your soul. It's time to embrace your emotions like a friend who cries with you without telling you to stand up. Feeling is part of the journey. And feeling everything, even the ugly, reminds you that you're still here. Breathing. Living. Feeling little by little more you.

Grieving the Lost Relationship: Stages and How to Navigate Them

They say that ruptures are not healed, they are crossed. And to go through them, you first have to understand that you are grieving. Yes, just like when you lose someone physically. Because, even if the other person is still alive and uploading stories on the beach as if nothing happened, for you that relationship died. And that duel deserves respect, time... and a healthy dose of compassion (preferably with yourself).

Not all people experience grief in the same way or in the same order, but there are some universal stages that are repeated like the messages you should never have sent at three in the morning. Here I present them to you with sincerity and a little humor, because if we don't laugh, we cry again.

1. Denial

"It can't be, I'm sure he's confused, he's going to come back, this is a test of the universe." At this stage you still check their last connection, analyze every word of the last message as if it were Morse code, and make mental lists of all the good things they had. Denying is a way of not facing the abyss, but it is also the gateway to everything else. Don't blame yourself. Just don't stay and live there.

2. Anger

Suddenly, you clearly see everything that you used to justify. What hurt, what you kept silent, what you ignored. And it is angry. Much. You get angry with yourself, with your ex, with your friends who "never told you anything", with the horoscope that promised you eternal love. This stage is powerful. Channel it: run, scream, write, dance reggaeton despite. But don't write to him. Please.

3. Negotiation

The most treacherous. "What if we talk?", "What if we are just friends?", "What if I change this or that?". Here the heart begins to make deals with logic to avoid feeling the emptiness. It's like an emotional auction where you offer parts of yourself so that the other person returns. Do not enter that tender. Real love is not negotiated with unilateral sacrifices.

4. Deep sadness

It's the downfall. Crying without explanation. Not wanting to get out of bed. The emptiness in the chest and the sad music at full volume. It is not a stage to accelerate or to deny. It's to embrace. This is where you really start to let go. Even if it hurts. Even if it seems like you're never going to get out. Surprise: you're going out. But first, you have to feel.

5. Acceptance

It's not that suddenly everything is peace and light. It doesn't hurt the same anymore. There is no longer any need to review their networks or imagine reconciliations. You start to see yourself in the mirror without that lost look. You regain your appetite for life. And even if there are still cloudy days, you know that you can go through them without falling apart. This stage does not come all at once. It comes in little pieces. But when it comes... It feels like coming home.

Navigating grief is an emotional journey without GPS. You're going to feel lost, you're going to go backwards, you're going to think you're over it, and then cry again over a silly thing. It is ok. It's not a race. It's a process. And every step, even the clumsiest, is leading you to a healthier place. You. Untethered. No dependencies. With the heart in reconstruction and dignity intact.

There are no shortcuts to pain

No matter how many "healing with wine" memes circulate, no matter how many friends tell you "go out with someone new" or no matter how many spiritual gurus promise to close cycles with a salt bath and three moonstones, the truth is this: pain has no shortcuts. There is no fast route, no secret path, no magic button to "forget everything and carry on as if nothing happened". And if there was, you would have already pressed it five times.

The pain is slow, heavy, and capricious. It arrives when you least expect it: in line at the supermarket, when watching a silly movie, when smelling the perfume I was wearing. And even if you want to avoid it, ignore it, or bury it under a mountain of activities, he finds a way to get noticed. Because what is not felt, is repeated. And what is repressed, rots.

Sometimes you want to run. Or anesthetizing yourself with distractions, empty dates, overwork, or motivational phrases that don't sink in. But skipping the pain is like trying to paint a broken wall without fixing it first: on the outside it looks like everything is fine, but on the inside, it keeps falling apart. And a cracked heart loves no better. Just love with fear.

Feeling hurts. A lot. But it also purifies. Crying is not defeat, it is drainage. Anger is not failure, it is defense. Tiredness is not a sign that you can't take it anymore, it's a warning that you need to stop. The pain is uncomfortable, yes. But he is also a teacher. It shows you what you gave too much, what you kept quiet out of fear, what you deserved and did not receive.

I'm not telling you that you like to suffer. I'm telling you that if you're going to go through this emotional fire, let it be to build back better. Don't skip the burning, because that's where the transformation lies. Don't settle for making up the wound. That you go deep, even if it burns.

There is no short way. But there is a way. And it is going step by step. Cry by crying. Breath by breath. Not to forget what you have experienced, but to let go of what no longer takes you anywhere. Pain is not the enemy. It's the door. Go through it. Even if it hurts. Even if it trembles. Even if it seems eternal. It will not be. You do.

Immediate coping techniques

When the heart breaks, the body panics. And no, you're not exaggerating: your chest closes, your throat gets knotted, your stomach seems to forget how to function. It's as if your entire nervous system decides to run away with your arms raised shouting "sentimental emergency!" Luckily, there are ways to calm that internal chaos before you end up crying in the dairy aisle with a bag of chips as a tissue.

Mindful Breathing: Your Emotional Emergency Button

It seems basic, but when you're in crisis, even breathing becomes a heroic act. Do this: inhale for a count of four, hold the air for another four, and exhale slowly for a count of six. Repeated. You don't need incense or whale music. Just your air. The breath activates the emergency brake in your body and tells your mind, "We're not safe yet, but we're not going to die for love either."

Mindfulness: being here, now, even if you don't want to

Your mind is probably in the past ("why did you tell me that?") or in the future ("what if I never find someone else?"). Mindfulness invites you to bring her back to this moment, where neither your ex-ex exists, nor anxiety has power. Observe your surroundings. The color of the sky, the sound of your surroundings, the smell of coffee. You don't have to reach enlightenment. Just reconnect with the present, that place where you still have power.

Healthy Distraction: Turning Off the Obsession Without Shutting Yourself Down

It's not about denying what you're feeling but about creating pauses so that you don't drown in the intensity. Watch a series that doesn't include happy couples every five minutes. Paint, even if you don't know how to draw a tree. Going for a walk aimlessly. Reorganize the stocking drawer. Calling someone who makes you laugh without asking you to "get over it." The idea is not to run away from pain, but to remind you that there is also life outside of sadness.

These tools don't solve grief, but they do give you a break. And sometimes, all you need to keep going is a breather. One deep, one present, one yours. Because, even if you can't control the emotional tremor, you can anchor yourself. And that, in the midst of the shipwreck, is already an act of self-love.

Avoiding destructive coping mechanisms (alcohol, drugs, impulsivity)

In the midst of spite, emotional chaos, and the internal rain that doesn't stop, it's tempting to seek quick relief. A drink "to calm the nerves", a night out "to forget", an impulsive message "just to see if he answers". Surprise: all that seems like a good idea at the moment... until you wake up the next day with more guilt than relief, more anxiety than clarity, and maybe with a story you'd rather not have starred in.

Alcohol promises to turn off the pain, but it only turns down the volume for a while. Then he raises it higher. Drugs offer a pause, but they don't cure, they just freeze. And what is frozen eventually melts. Impulsive decisions, such as writing to your ex at two in the morning or looking for "closure" in someone who never even thanked you, only prolong the wound and feed self-deception.

There are also other more subtle, but equally destructive escapes: throwing yourself into work until you forget to eat, dating someone new just so you don't feel lonely, pretending on social media that you're better off than you are. All of this is emotional anesthesia, and like all anesthesia, it loses its effect. And when it does, the pain comes back with interest.

It is not a question of judging yourself if you have already fallen into any of these mechanisms. It's about stopping the wheel before it hits you. It's about asking yourself an honest question: does this really relieve me, or does it just distract me from the void? Because it's one thing to indulge yourself, and quite another to use that pleasure as an excuse not to look at what hurts.

You're grieving. And although it seems that there is no way to sustain it, there is. But you are not at the bottom of a bottle, or in the arms of someone who does not know you, or in decisions made from emotional hunger. Healing is not covering the wound with glitter. It's cleaning it, even if it hurts. It's looking at you in the face, even if you don't like what you see.

You don't need to escape. You need care. Not from others, but from you. Because no one else can rescue you from the abyss if you decide to stay there out of habit yourself. And you deserve more than surviving on impulses. You deserve to heal with awareness, even if it takes time. Even if it hurts. Even if it is difficult to look straight ahead. Because when you make it, and you're going to make it, you're not going to need distractions to feel at peace. You're going to be at peace.

The importance of crying and venting

Crying is not a sign of weakness, nor a setback in the process, nor a shame that must be hidden in the bathroom with the shower on so that no one hears. Crying is medicine. A primitive, powerful and deeply human way of letting go of what the body can no longer carry. If the soul had escape valves, it would be the eyes.

There are those who tell you to "don't cry anymore", as if shedding tears were an emotional crime. But don't cry for what you lost, they say. How absurd. And why not? If it hurt you, if it marked you, if you gave love, time, illusions. Of course you're going to cry. You cry because it matters. Because what is gone does not leave without leaving a void. And because emotions don't evaporate just by gritting your teeth and carrying on as usual.

Crying cleanses. Not only the eyes, but the inner corners where anger, sadness, and frustration accumulate. After crying, the body rests. The mind clears. The heart beats with fewer knots. It's not that the pain goes away, but it becomes more manageable. It's like emptying the glass a little so that it doesn't overflow.

And we don't always cry with tears. Sometimes they cry in the form of silence. Insomnia. From unsent messages. Of playlists that break more than comfort. Crying can also be sitting alone and acknowledging out loud, "I'm not okay." You don't need an audience, or wise words, or permission. Just give you space to feel.

Venting is not "dramatizing". It's honoring what you're experiencing. Keeping the pain to yourself doesn't make you strong, it makes you explode inside later on. So cry when you need to. Shout if necessary. Write down what you can't say. Break leaves, not hearts. But don't swallow it all believing that you're going to heal without hitting rock bottom.

Tears don't make you weak. They make you real. They make you brave. And most of all, they remind you that feeling is not a curse. It's part of the way back to you. A wet one, yes. But also profoundly liberating.

Seek Support: Friends, Family, Therapy

Even if you feel alone, you are not alone. And you don't have to do this without help, without witnesses, without someone to pass you a tissue or, better yet, a scoop of ice cream and a look that says "I understand you" without needing to say anything. The shared pain does not go away, but it becomes lighter. As if by distributing it, your heart breathes a little better.

Your friends, those who already knew that this romance was heading for shipwreck for a long time, can be your first lifeline. They're not there to say "I told you so" (well, sometimes I did, but with love), but to hear you repeat the same story five times in a row without judging you, to see you cry with a swollen face and keep saying you're beautiful, and to remind you of who you are when you forget.

Your family can be another anchor, even if sometimes they don't understand all the details. Maybe they don't know what to say, maybe their way of supporting is to make you soup or ask you a thousand times if you've already eaten. Never mind. The point is to surround yourself with people who take care of you without asking you for explanations. That gives you space but also hugs you if necessary.

And if you feel that no one can sustain what you have inside, or that your emotions overwhelm you beyond what those close to you can have, there is therapy. Seeking professional help is not a luxury, it is an act of self-love. It says to yourself: "this hurts me so much that I need a guide to go through it without getting lost". A therapist isn't going to erase your suffering, but they're going to give you tools, perspective, and a safe space to rebuild yourself.

Asking for help doesn't make you strong any less. It makes you human. Because we were not born to heal in silence or to carry everything without support. Sometimes the bravest thing is not to go forward alone, but to reach out and say "I can't take it anymore". And when you do, you discover that the world doesn't fall apart... opens. And in that opening, you begin to find your way back to yourself. More accompanied. More sustained. More alive.

What is zero contact and why is it crucial?

Zero contact is not a childish strategy, nor a way to "make you jealous", nor a manipulation technique to make your ex miss you. It's an act of emotional survival. It's about cutting off all kinds of communication with that person: no messages, no calls, no "I reacted to their story unintentionally", no "I went in just to see if they had uploaded something new". Nothing. Zero. Zero is zero. Even if your finger trembles when you see that it's online. Even if your brain tells you that maybe just one message doesn't hurt. Warning: it does.

Why is it so important? Because while you continue to have access to their life, you don't get out of yours. Every message is a relapse. Every attempt at "I just want to know how he's doing" is actually a way to keep alive an illusion that has already been broken. Zero contact is not punishment. It is closure. It is protection. It's the wall you need to build as your heart rearms itself with new pieces.

Being in contact with your ex, even passively, is like trying to heal a wound while still scratching yourself. It never closes. It never stops hurting. And the worst enemy of grief is misplaced hope.

The one that feeds on likes, ambiguous messages, "maybe he still loves me". No. If I wanted you well, you would be fine. Period.

Zero contact is not easy. There is a part of you that wants to continue knowing, that clings to the "what if it changes?", that looks for absurd excuses to write to it ("I just wanted to warn you that your cat looks at me ugly in my dreams"). But what you're really looking for isn't information, it's validation. And it's time to stop looking for it in someone who didn't know how to give it to you.

Yes, at first it feels like an amputation. Because it is. But it is also the beginning of reconstruction. Because only in silence is the truth settled. Only from a distance can the whole story be seen. And only without interference do you begin to hear the most important voice of all: yours.

So when in doubt, remember this: zero contact isn't about him, it's about you. About your peace, your clarity and your rebirth. It is the red button that is pressed with fear, but that activates power. Yours. The one who no longer asks for love where there is none. The one who is not satisfied with crumbs. The one who, this time, chooses to truly heal.

Types of contact (direct, indirect, social media)

When we talk about zero contact, it's not enough to block the number and take a deep breath. The ex, like cockroaches, always finds creative ways to reappear. That's why it's important to know all the types of contact you should cut off or avoid so that the healing process doesn't become a game of snakes and ladders where you go up one day and fall five steps the next.

1. Direct contact: the most obvious, but also the most difficult to let go.

Here we are talking about calls, text messages, emails, video calls, or that classic "I saw you around here and I wanted to greet you". You don't have to be Sherlock Holmes to know that as long as you keep talking to your ex, even if it's "as friends", you're not closing anything. Each interaction opens the wound again, leaves you with more doubts than certainties and often with self-esteem on the ground. Zero is zero. Even if he writes "just to know how you are" or "I remembered you because of this song". Let it be remembered in silence.

2. Indirect contact: the most deceitful of all.

This is the famous "I asked his cousin how he was" or "I saw in his profile that he went to the same bar where we went". It also includes covert surveillance, talking about him with acquaintances, asking your friends to "just look at him to see who he's with" or reading between the lines every sad song he uploads to Spotify. This kind of contact seems harmless, but it fuels obsession and keeps hope alive rather than closing the loop. And yes, blocking also includes not spying from fake accounts. You're not the CIA.

3. Contact on social networks: the emotional buffet that you have to stop visiting.

The networks are a cruel trap. You see what he wants to show, not what he really feels. And of course, there he is: laughing, going out, seemingly happy without you. That tears you apart. But it's not real. Or not at all. And even if it were, why continue exposing yourself to that voluntary visual punishment? Delete, block, or mute. And not out of spite, but out of peace of mind. Because seeing their stories is not innocent. It is self-betrayal.

There is also emotional contact disguised as spiritual contact: that "I dreamed it last night, I'm sure he's thinking of me" or "today I heard our song, it must be a sign from the universe". No, it's not. It's your mind looking for excuses not to let go. Be grateful for the memory... and release it as well.

Anything that connects you to your ex, whether by words, by sight, by gossip, or by selective intuition, is contact. And all contact is regression. You don't need to know how it's doing. You need to know how you are. You don't need signals. You need silence. The kind of silence that doesn't hurt but heals. And it only comes when you close all the doors... even emotional ones.

How to implement it: Block, mute, avoid commonplaces

You've already understood that zero contact is crucial. Now comes the difficult part: to apply it without your hand or your dignity trembling. Because it's one thing to say "I'm not going to talk to him anymore", and quite another to not write to him when you see that he uploaded a story in which he appears with someone else... Smiling. So here is a practical and straightforward guide to putting zero contact into operation in an effective and, above all, protective way.

Block without guilt or explanation

Blocking is not an act of revenge or drama, it is a decision of personal care. You don't need to give notice. You don't have to send one last message like "I'm leaving, take care of yourself". You just do it. You block the number, WhatsApp, Instagram, Facebook, email and any channel through which that person can reappear to leave you emotional crumbs. It is not cruelty, it is an instinct of self-preservation. If someone left open wounds, they cannot have free access to your peace.

Mute everything around you (and what reminds you of it)

Do you have mutual friends? Silence them. Do you follow his aunt who always comments "my beautiful boy"? Outside. Do you skip a song they used to listen to? Goodbye. At first it may seem exaggerated, but it is not about erasing the past but about protecting the present. Every little reminder is an emotional mini-stab. And you don't need to collect knives when you're trying to close wounds.

Avoid platitudes: Your emotional GPS needs reconfiguration

Stop showing up "casually" by that café where you used to go, the street where you live, the bar where your friend works, or any place where your neurons say "maybe I'll see it". You're not looking for coffee. You're looking for attention crumbs. And you are not made to beg for love in spaces that no longer do you good. Change your route, discover new places, also unfollow the corners that no longer nourish you.

Implementing zero contact takes courage. Not because it's radical, but because it goes against all your emotional impulses. But those impulses no longer serve you. They tied you up. And this is the time to let go firmly. Do it with the same love that you once delivered. Only this time, direct it towards you. Because when you protect yourself from what hurts you, you are already beginning to heal. And that really deserves a block... and applause.

The "buts" and exceptions (children, shared goods): Strategies to minimize them

We know that, in an ideal world, zero contact would be as simple as "block and forget." But there are cases where reality messes with dirty shoes and tells you: "You can't disappear because you have a child together, a dog, a mortgage or a car in your name." And that's where the grief gets complicated, because nipping in the bud is not always possible. But be careful: just because you can't cut it all the way doesn't mean you can't protect yourself.

If there are children involved: limited, clear and neutral communication

Having a child together doesn't force you to remain emotionally available to your ex. What is needed is logistics, not affection. Create communication agreements that are exclusively about the child: schedules, medical decisions, school activities. No "how are you?" or "I remembered you because our son has your smile". Use apps designed for co-parenting or written messages that leave a record. Short, objective and unadorned conversations. You are not their friend, nor their confidant. You are the mother of his child. Point.

If there are shared assets: divide and give what is possible

When there are material things in between—an apartment, bills, debts, furniture, or the microwave you bought together—it's best to resolve it as soon as possible. If you can split without drama, do it quickly. If not, it involves a neutral third party: a lawyer, a mediator or someone sane who does not take sides. Avoid face-to-face meetings as much as possible. Don't go picking things up alone. Don't sit down "to talk" because that usually ends with tears, theories, and sometimes kisses that confuse them more. You're not for soap opera scenes.

Set firm limits, even if your soul trembles

Exceptions are not excuses to open the door to emotional disorder. If they have to speak, let it be in a clear channel, in writing and without embellishments. No night calls "because the child misses". If they ask you to speak in person, ask yourself: is it strictly necessary? Or are they looking for an excuse to sneak into your present disguised as responsibility?

And if they still live together (because life is sometimes cruel)

Define physical and emotional spaces. Sleep in another room. Speak only what is necessary. Don't share your emotions with someone who no longer knows how to hold them. And she works, daily, to get out of that coexistence as soon as possible. The longer you prolong the "we live together, but we are nothing anymore", the later your healing begins.

You can't avoid all ties. But you can reconfigure them. It is not about being cold, but about being clear. It's not about getting revenge, it's about protecting yourself. And while there may be "buts," remember this: the priority now isn't your comfort, nor shared nostalgia. It's your peace. And that admits no exceptions.

Who were you before this relationship? Rediscovering your identity

When a relationship ends, it's not just the loss of the other person that hurts... The loss of yourself also hurts. Because, without realizing it, you were giving up space, adjusting your tastes, keeping things quiet, adapting. And now that he's gone, you find yourself in front of the mirror asking yourself, "And what did I want? What did I like to do before all this? What did I dream when I was still dreaming alone?"

It's normal to feel lost. During a relationship, especially if it was intense or long, your identity is mixed with that of the other. It becomes a "we" that eclipses the "I." You leave hobbies, you postpone plans, you choose movies that don't interest you, you go to places you never liked so much. And the worst thing is that many times you don't do it out of obligation, but out of love. By routine. Out of habit. Until one day you no longer know how yours is the life you are living.

Now that you're alone, it's not a punishment. It is an invitation. To look inside you for that version that was waiting in a corner. The one who danced without thinking about whether you were doing it right. The one who laughed alone. The one who wrote, sang, went out, or simply felt enough without having to show it all the time. Rediscovering yourself is reconnecting with that woman who didn't need to be chosen to know that she was worthy.

Remember. What did you do before that relationship that made you feel alive? What did you abandon without realizing it? Who were you with without needing to explain yourself? Recovering your identity is not going back to the past, it is bringing to the present the best of you that you had forgotten. And maybe discover new parts too, because every pain opens doors that you didn't dare to cross before.

Make lists. Resume activities. Try new things without asking yourself if he would like them. Change your room, your clothes, your music. Not because you need to be someone else, but because you are coming back to yourself, with new wounds, yes, but also with more truth. More strength. More clarity on what you don't want to repeat.

You're not a better half. You're not a project to complete. You are a whole woman, even if at times you don't feel that way. And now that the "we" is behind us, it's time to reconnect with the most important person in your life: you. No filters. No permits. No apologies. Because rediscovering yourself is not just part of the process... It's the real happy ending.

Hobbies, passions and forgotten interests

One of the silent consequences of many relationships is the forgetting of what once made you glow inside. Those little rituals you loved, the activities that filled your soul, the dreams you wrote down in notebooks and then let them dust because "there was no time" or "they were no longer a priority". And now, that love is gone, you find yourself facing the void asking yourself: "And what did I do when I was happy without depending on anyone?"

Maybe you used to paint, even if it was just doodles, you wrote without anyone reading you, you danced with a broom as a couple or you sang as if you were part of a musical. Maybe you were fascinated by crime documentaries, aimless walks, classes on something useless but funny, or daydreaming about opening a café with books and cats. Things that you did just because, because you liked them, because they made you feel like you.

When you're in a relationship, many times those passions fade little by little. It's not that someone comes to take them off, it's that you yourself, without realizing it, are letting them rust. Because there are outings as a couple. Because there are shared schedules. Because you are more aware of the other than of yourself. And so, what was once fire becomes silent ash.

This is the perfect time to sweep up those ashes and stoke the embers again. Pick up where you left off. Try what you never dared to try. Not to impress anyone, not to forcibly heal the heart, but because you deserve it. Because if you are going to rebuild yourself, it is better to do it from pleasure, from curiosity, from that corner of yours where no one else is in charge.

Make a list of everything you ever loved to do. And if you don't remember anything, try new things as if you were a teenager with a new heart. Take absurd classes, learn something useless, go to museums, even if you don't understand art, enroll in yoga, even if you're more plank than the floor. Do it all. And do it without waiting for approval.

Your passions were not hobbies: they were bridges to your essence. And if you stopped crossing them, today is the day to rebuild them. Because in the midst of mourning, crying, rebuilding, there is also room for joy. For laughter. To come back to you through what always connected you to your inner fire. Your ex left. But your desire, your ideas, your creative energy are still there. And they're waiting for you to choose them. This time, without letting go for anyone.

Define your personal values and goals

After a breakup, there's a question that begins to echo inside you like an insistent little bell: "What now?" And while the temptation is to fill that void with distractions, the real magic happens when you stop and ask yourself, "What do I really want? What is important to me, without it, without us, without excuses?" Because this is your opportunity to return to yourself, not as one who returns to the known, but as one who discovers a new territory with more awakened eyes.

Defining your values is like fine-tuning your internal compass. They are those non-negotiable ideas that sustain you even when everything falls apart. Perhaps respect, freedom, honesty, loyalty, authenticity, peace. How many times did you sacrifice them to keep the relationship afloat? How many times did you betray yourself a little bit so as not to make you uncomfortable? Now is the time to get them back, to say, "Yes, this. Not anymore. This never again."

And then come your goals. Not the shared ones, not the ones that were built in the plural, but yours. What dreams did you postpone? What goals did you have before falling in love? What new goals have been born from this process? Maybe you want to move, finish your studies, open that business you always imagined, write a book, adopt a cat or a parrot, travel alone, heal your body, speak another language, or simply learn to be with yourself without fear. All that is valid. All that counts.

This is your time to write your personal manifesto. Not to hang it on the wall, but to remind you of it every time sadness wants to drag you into what no longer was. You're not here just to survive a breakup. You are here to rebuild your life from what does resonate with you. From what moves you. From what makes sense to you, even if no one else understands it.

Your values and your goals are your north. And the clearer you are, the less likely you are to return to what made you deviate. Because a person who knows what he wants does not settle for less. Not with half-hearted love, nor with relationships that hurt more than they heal.

So take this time not as a punishment, but as a fallen compass that gets back into position. And remember it's not just about defining who you are without that relationship. It's about choosing, with self-love, who you're going to be from now on.

And this time, that decision doesn't depend on anyone but you.

The importance of autonomy and emotional independence

One of the great lessons of a breakup – after the crying, the sad nights and the conversations with your unqualified psychologist friend – is this: you can't keep handing over the keys to your emotional well-being to someone else. Because when your mood depends on whether they answer you or not, if they upload a sad or happy story, if they love you or ignore you, you are living on an emotional tightrope that sooner or later breaks. And you always fall, not them.

Emotional autonomy doesn't mean locking yourself in a cave and swearing that you'll never love again. It means learning to be with yourself without feeling incomplete. It's recognizing that you can grieve, miss, and heal... without begging for answers. That you can have ties, yes, but without your identity depending on them. That you can be in a couple without becoming a satellite revolving around each other as if your existence had no orbit of its own.

When you're emotionally dependent, it's all about fear: fear of them leaving, fear of not liking them, fear of not being enough. And that fear makes you give in, shut up, justify things that hurt you. But when you cultivate your emotional independence, you don't need anyone to constantly confirm you, because you have already chosen yourself. Not as a plan B. As a priority.

Being autonomous does not mean needing anyone. It means knowing that, even if you lack them, you don't break. It means that you can be alone without being empty. That you know how to comfort yourself, set limits, please yourself and ask for help without feeling that your world is ending if you are not answered at once. It is to build within yourself the refuge that you used to look for outside.

And no, it is not achieved from one day to the next. It is a constant work. It's looking at your wounds and deciding that you're not going to use anyone else as a band-aid. That you will heal from the root, with time, with compassion, with firm decisions. Because when you hold yourself, the world doesn't feel so threatening anymore. You no longer choose from lack, but from desire. You no longer beg for love, you share it.

Emotional independence is that muscle that you don't see, but you can tell. In how you speak, in how you decide, in how you take care of yourself.

And although it is built alone, it transforms all your bonds. Because when you no longer need to be loved to feel alive, then you are ready to truly love. Free. Whole. Unswerving.

Physical health: Food, exercise, sleep

When the heart is in ruins, the body feels it. You lose your appetite or eat the world in the form of potato chips. You wake up at three in the morning with your heart racing, dreaming that your ex regrets it, or worse, that he is happy without you. And exercise... Well, if you lifted anything this week, it was the bag of sweet bread. And that's okay. At first, the body goes into "romantic survival" mode. But you can't stay and live there.

Your physical health is not a luxury, it is the support of your entire emotional process. Taking care of it doesn't mean getting into the gym and yelling in the air while doing vengeful squats. It means starting, little by little, to remind your body that it is safe, that it does not need to live on alert, that it deserves to feel good, even if the heart is learning to beat again.

Food: No More Spite Diet

If you can't swallow even air, start with things that are soft, nutritious, and warm. Soups, fruits, smoothies, whatever doesn't turn your stomach, but gives you energy. And if you're taking refuge in sugar as if it were your new lover, don't beat yourself up, but don't sabotage yourself either. Balance does not come in a day, it comes with small decisions that tell you "I care, even if I am broken".

Exercise: Moving so you don't get stuck

You don't have to run a marathon or become an emotional athlete. Just walk, dance alone in your room, do yoga with a non-judgmental app, or just stretch. Movement takes the pain out of the body. It changes your focus. It reminds you that you are still here, in this body that you may have forgotten while you were busy loving someone else.

Dream: Your Sacred Refuge

Getting a good night's sleep after a breakup may seem like science fiction. You are haunted by memories, questions, silences. But your mind needs rest to process what you're experiencing. Turn off screens before bed, create a gentle routine (even if it's a shower and tea), and avoid staring at breakup memes at two in the morning. If insomnia persists, don't normalize it: seek help, look for tools, but don't sacrifice your nights.

Taking care of your body is a radical act of self-love. It tells you your nervous system: "Don't worry, we're not going to die from this." Because it's not about having a flat stomach or the perfect eight hours of sleep. It's about living in yourself again. To treat you with the same affection you once had with someone who is no longer there. This time, the surrender is to you. And believe me: your body will thank you. And your soul, too.

Mental health: Meditation, therapy if needed

A breakup not only breaks your heart, it also shakes your mind as if someone has shuffled your thoughts with their eyes closed. Suddenly, you don't know if you're coming or going, if you're sad, angry, confused, or all at the same time. The nights become eternal, insomnia sets in as a tenant, and your brain decides to binge-watch catastrophic thoughts at three in the morning. That's where your mental health needs more than a self-help meme. It needs real care. Constant. Loving.

Meditation: turning off the noise to listen to yourself

You don't need to be a Tibetan monk or learn Sanskrit. Meditating is not leaving the mind blank (not even the Dalai Lama with Wi-Fi can do that). It's sitting for a few minutes, breathing, seeing what you feel without fighting with it. It is giving yourself a moment a day to be with yourself without demands. There are thousands of free guides, apps, and videos that can help you get started. The important thing is not to make it perfect, it is to do it. It is letting silence do what words cannot: order internal chaos from within.

Therapy: a safe space without filters or judgments

Talking to a person trained to help you is not a sign that you are wrong, it is a sign that you are taking charge. A good therapist won't tell you what you want to hear, but she's going to walk you to see what you need to understand. It will give you tools to get out of the labyrinth, to rebuild your self-esteem, to stop looking for answers where there are no longer questions. And if you feel that you can't do it alone, don't take it as defeat. It's courage. It's maturity. It's real self-care.

And if you can't access therapy now, there are other doors

Read emotional psychology books, listen to podcasts that don't romanticize suffering, write down what you're feeling without censorship, talk to someone who will listen to you without interrupting. All of that helps, too. The important thing is not to stay silent with the pain in your throat. Not everything heals itself. And not everything is overcome by pretending that it no longer hurts.

Your mental health is the foundation of everything else. You can eat healthily, exercise, and get eight hours of sleep, but if your mind is stuck in the "why did he leave me?" the body is still going to be at war. So breathe. Speech. Seek help if you need it. You're not crazy. You are healing. And that, although it may seem invisible, is the bravest act of all.

Personal Development: Learning Something New, Reading, Growing

After a breakup, there's a gap. Emotional, mental, even logistical. Suddenly you have too many afternoons, thoughts and songs that no longer sound the same. The good thing is that that space that was once occupied by a relationship that no longer exists can now be filled with something infinitely more powerful: your growth. Because healing is also building. And one of the most beautiful (and useful) ways to heal is to evolve.

Learning something new: don't let your broken heart take away your hunger to learn

It's not about becoming a multitasking superwoman just to prove that you're "better than ever." It is about giving your mind new routes to walk on. Learn to cook, edit videos, knit, program, dance bachata or speak Japanese. It doesn't matter what. What matters is that you do it for yourself. That you discover dormant talents or new passions that have nothing to do with your ex or the past. Learning something reminds you that your story isn't over: it's just being rewritten.

Reading: Your brain needs comfort (and adventures) too

A good book can be a refuge, a mirror or a ladder. You can read novels that transport you away from your sadness, essays that make you think differently, poetry that embraces your soul, or self-exploration books that help you understand why you keep looking for love where there is none. The important thing is to choose texts that nourish you, not sink you. No romantic stories with perfect endings if that's going to leave you crying when you close the page. Read what feeds you. Not what punishes you.

Growing: not as pressure, but as choice

This is the perfect time to look honestly. What patterns do you repeat in your relationships? What wounds still guide your decisions? What parts of you do you need to reinforce so that you don't go back to the same place? Growing up hurts, of course. But it hurts differently than the pain of a breakup. It hurts like a growth spurt. Like when you're building something that's worthwhile: yourself.

Personal development isn't an Instagram fad or a to-do list to brag about. It's a quiet commitment to you. It is giving you tools so that next time you do not choose from fear, but from fullness. It shows you that you don't need a perfect heart to move forward. Only one willing.

And if someone asks you what you're doing with your life now that you're alone, you can answer without fear: growing. That it is not fast, or easy, or always glamorous. But it's real. And no one can take it away from you. Not even your ex.

Create a routine that nourishes you

After a breakup, the days get messy. The bed becomes a trench, the hours pass senselessly and even washing your hair feels like an impossible mission. But in the midst of that emotional chaos, creating a routine isn't just a way to bring order, it's a way to get back to yourself. A nutritious routine is not rigid or demanding. It's soft, flexible and tailor-made for you. Not so that you are productive at all costs, but so that every day reminds you that you deserve care.

Mornings with intention, not in a hurry

Start by giving yourself ten minutes before touching the cell phone. Breathe. Stretch. Drink water. Play music that won't tear you apart. You can write a couple of lines about how you feel or just say to yourself "I take care of myself today". You don't need a thousand-step ritual. Just something that anchors you to the present before your mind starts racing into the past.

Foods That Are Punished, That Are Punished

It's not about eating perfectly but about choosing foods that make you feel alive and not guilty. Eat calmly, even if it's alone. Make the act of feeding not a formality or an excuse to fill in the gaps. Preparing something delicious is a simple but powerful form of self-love.

Daily movement, even if it's minimal

Walking, stretching, dancing in pajamas, doing yoga with a free app. You're not training for the emotional Olympics. You're just helping your body release tension and remind it that it can still move freely. Sometimes, twenty minutes of movement does more for you than three hours of mental drama.

Moments to connect with you

Block out one space a day, even if it's fifteen minutes, just for you. Reading, writing, meditating, drawing, doing something you like or just looking out the window without thinking about anything. Don't underestimate the power of those quiet moments. They are balm for the soul.

Nights that invite rest, not mental punishment

Avoid checking their networks before sleeping. Don't play sad music as if you were the protagonist of a dramatic video clip. Create a simple routine: a hot shower, a tea, a gratitude list, or a light reading. Your body needs to know that the day can end peacefully, even if the heart continues with stitches.

A routine that nourishes you is not an obligation. It's a daily "I've got me" statement. And the more you hold on to your daily life, the less room anxiety has to clutter yourself. Because in the end, what heals is not always the big gestures, but the small acts of care repeated with love. Every day. Even if it costs. Even if it hurts. Even if at first, you're just surviving. That routine is also part of your rebirth. And you're worth it. Every day.

Set healthy boundaries in your relationships

After a breakup, one of the most urgent (and most uncomfortable) lessons is this: you need boundaries. Not walls, not impenetrable emotional barriers, but real, conscious, loving boundaries. Because part of healing is not only to stop missing the one who left, but to stop betraying yourself every time someone crosses a line, and you smile like nothing happened.

A healthy boundary is a silent statement that says: this is me, this I don't overlook, this I don't allow anymore. It is not coldness. It is not selfishness. It's clarity. And clarity takes care of you, orders you, gives you peace. Learning to set boundaries isn't about pushing others away, it's about getting closer to yourself.

1. You don't have to justify what makes you uncomfortable

If something bothers you, you don't need to explain your history of trauma, astrology, or entire childhood for it to have value. It is enough that it makes you uncomfortable for it to deserve to be treated. No is no. Point. Even if it seems exaggerated to the other person. You are not there to convince anyone to respect you.

2. Silence is also a limit

Do not respond to unnecessary messages, do not follow conversations that wear you down, do not go every time someone needs you as if you were an emotional ambulance. The silence also says "that's it." Don't underestimate it. Used with intention, it can be firmer than a thousand speeches.

3. Putting distance is not being a bad person

Sometimes you have to stay away from people who don't know or don't want to treat you well. Even if they are family. Even if they are friends for years. Even if they tell you "you have changed". Of course you changed. You stopped putting up with what you were silent about before. You're not being cruel. You're being clear.

4. Learn to say no without making a thousand excuses

I don't want to. I can't. It doesn't do me any good. It is not born to me. I don't need to explain. This type of "no" is going to be difficult at first, especially if you were one of those who said yes for fear of making you uncomfortable. But it's the kind of noise that sets you free. And it takes care of you. And it reminds you that no one is above your peace.

5. Limits are not asked, they are set

It is not a matter of begging for respect. It's about holding it yourself. If someone insists on crossing your boundaries, you don't need to fight or give eternal speeches. You retire. You change the tone. You take a distance. And you do it with your head held high. Not guilty. With conviction.

Setting boundaries is the most practical way to love yourself. It is not a question of imposing them with anger, but of keeping them firmly. Make it clear where the other ends and where you begin. Because not everyone who loves you takes care of you. But you can. And from now on, you're going to do it. Fearless. No drama. With self-love as a flag.

Meeting New People (Not Romantically): Groups, Activities

After a breakup, it's easy to fall into the trap of thinking that you'll only heal when someone new looks at you again like your ex did (or like you thought they did). But not every new beginning has to do with romance. Sometimes, what you need most is to reconnect with other people through laughter, curiosity, shared interests... No kisses, no expectations, no dramas.

Meeting new people without the filter of "is something wrong?" is a breath of fresh air. It reminds you that the world is bigger than a broken relationship. That there's life beyond dating apps, and that you can share genuine moments without being emotionally on fire.

Stakeholders: Your tribe is out there, but it doesn't arrive alone

Look for spaces that bring together people with similar tastes: writing workshops, book clubs, hiking groups, cooking classes, meditation circles, community theater, urban gardening, pottery classes, or even online courses with active forums. It doesn't matter if you're shy or you arrive alone. Most of them are there for the same reason: to share something different, to break the routine, to add.

Volunteering: the perfect antidote to emotional isolation

Helping others is one of the most beautiful ways to help yourself. You can collaborate in animal shelters, food banks, libraries, activities with children or ecological programs. There you will meet people with sensitivity, commitment and, best of all, without the need to talk about the ex or pretend that you are fine. Just be. And adding. And let yourself be surprised.

Cultural events and express workshops: try without committing

Sometimes it's best to just try. Going to an art fair, a chat in a café, and a weekend course. Something that doesn't force you to keep going if you don't like it, but that gives you the impetus to get out of the house and expose yourself to the world. You don't need big links at first. Only new scenarios where not everything smells of the past.

Healthy digital spaces: yes, they also exist

Well-used social networks, thematic communities, groups on topics that you are passionate about. Yes, you can meet interesting people on the internet without ending up emotionally entangled. The key is purpose, not the urgency to fill a void.

Going out into the world without looking for a partner, just for the pleasure of belonging to something bigger than your pain, is an act of courage. And it reminds you of something very powerful: you are not alone. You never were. Only now, at last, you're ready to look beyond the broken mirror. And to find yourself, too, in others. Unhurried. No armor. No need for romance to feel alive again.

The difference between support and dependency

After a breakup, it's normal to feel like you're missing the floor. That you need to talk to someone, hold on to whoever will listen to you, that someone tells you what to do when you don't even know how to get up. And yes, seeking support is healthy, necessary, and vital. But beware: support is not the same as dependence. One holds you up. The other suffocates you.

Support is companionship, not salvation. It's when you can talk to your friends, cry with your sister, consult with your therapist, or cuddle your dog without expecting them to figure out your life for you. It is when you feel containment without losing autonomy. You can share your pain without someone else carrying it. You can listen to advice without handing over the helm of your process to anyone. Support is that invisible network that holds you up... but it does not walk for you.

Dependency, on the other hand, is when you can't breathe if that person doesn't respond to you. When you need constant approval for every decision. When you don't know who you are outside the bond. When you make someone your emotional center, your only source of stability, your "everything." And that, even if it comes disguised as love or friendship, is a prison that disguises itself as a refuge.

To be emotionally dependent on someone is to ask them to take care of you as if you were fragile. To support you is to know that you are broken, yes, but in reconstruction. A supportive person gives you space, not control. It listens to you, but it doesn't direct you. It comforts you, but it doesn't cancel you out. And you, by leaning on yourself, keep power over your process.

The key difference? Support makes you stronger. Dependence weakens you. One connects you to yourself. The other disconnects you from you.

You're in a vulnerable moment, yes. But that doesn't mean you need to give yourself completely over to another human being in order to feel safe. What you need is to surround yourself with those who remind you of your strength when you forget it. Of those who do not solve your life but walk by your side while you rebuild it.

Support yourself, of course. He cries on sincere shoulders. Ask for help. But never forget about yourself in the process. Because no one is going to save you like you can. And when you do, from support and not from dependence, you will feel something incredible: freedom. And that is not negotiable.

Reflecting on the relationship: What did I learn?

After a breakup, there comes a moment when the crying subsides, the drama wears away, and the silence begins to make room for an uncomfortable but powerful question: what did I learn from all this? And it is not a matter of looking for the positive side of pain out of obligation, or of turning suffering into poetry at once, but of looking back honestly and taking something valuable from a story that has already ended.

Maybe you learned what you're no longer willing to tolerate. Perhaps you understood that it is not enough to love it also takes respect, reciprocity, presence, truth. You may have discovered how much you adapted to fit into something that left you no room to breathe. Or how much you abandoned yourself for fear of being alone. All of that counts, too. And a lot.

Learning does not mean justifying what hurt you. It means acknowledging the signs you ignored, the boundaries you didn't set, the times you betrayed yourself in the name of "we." It means seeing dynamics with clearer eyes, not to punish you, but to grow. Because no one comes out of love unscathed, but no one also comes out the same. And if you can't avoid the blow, at least you can choose what you do with what's left.

Perhaps you also learned beautiful things: that you are capable of giving yourself, of betting on a bond, of building from affection. That your ability to love is still alive, even if someone has not known how to value it. That you can trust again, to feel, to share. That love was not a mistake, even if the end hurt.

Ask yourself honestly: what parts of me grew? What wounds were there before? What red flags did I overlook for fear of abandonment? What did I learn about my way of loving and being loved? Not to reproach you, but not to repeat the cycle with a new name.

Reflection does not come all at once. It comes in waves, sometimes laughing, sometimes tearing, sometimes in the middle of a song or in casual conversation. But when it comes to something changes you stop looking at the relationship with nostalgia or anger, and you start to see it as a hard teacher, yes... but necessary.

Not all relationships are made to stay. Some come just to show you what you still need to heal, what you deserve and what you are no longer going to allow. If you learned that, then it wasn't in vain. It was a lesson. It was transit. It was part of your story. And now, with everything I learned, comes the most important part: writing the new one. With you as the protagonist. Without repeating what you already understood. And without letting go of what you finally discovered about yourself.

Find negative patterns in your relationships

One of the most powerful things you can do after a breakup—and also one of the most uncomfortable—is to look in the unfiltered emotional mirror and ask yourself: What do I tend to repeat in my relationships? Because no matter how much the face of the exchanges, if the emotional script is the same, the ending will also be.

Negative patterns are not coincidences of fate or romantic bad luck. They are repetitions that are born from old wounds, mistaken beliefs or misunderstood needs. And if you don't find them, you end up attracting the same kind of story with a different name and new perfume.

Do you always choose emotionally unavailable people? Do you find it difficult to set limits and end up giving more than you receive? Do you confuse intensity with love? Do you get hooked up with someone who needs to be "saved", and you put on the heroin cape? Do you tolerate disrespect because "no one is perfect"? Do you cling to the little for fear of being left with nothing?

Those are all patterns. And they don't break until you see them clearly and without excuses. The key is to recognize that you also took part in the dynamic. Not to blame you, but to empower you. Because if you are part of the cycle, you can also choose to get out of it.

Make a brutally honest list of what was repeated in your past relationships. What did you tolerate in silence? What did you ignore, even though you knew it would hurt you? What part of you looking for in others what you didn't know how to give yourself? It's uncomfortable, yes. But it is the beginning of emotional freedom.

And once you find them, name them. Write them down. Read them. Speak to them out loud if you need to. The more aware you make them, the less likely you are to fall back into them by inertia. Because it's not about promising that you won't make mistakes again. It's about recognizing where you were choosing from... and choosing differently.

Healing is not erasing what has been experienced. It is to understand it. It's telling you: I already understood why I chose that way, but now I'm no longer that version of me that conformed, that kept quiet, that got lost. Because once you see the pattern, you can't hide it anymore. And with that awareness, you're that much closer to building relationships where you don't have to beg for what you now know you deserve.

Forgiving (yourself and your ex, if possible and healthy)

The word forgiveness sounds nice in theory, but when you're heartbroken and a mental list of wounds still throbbing, the last thing you want is to "let go with love." Because, let's be honest, sometimes you want to let go with a verbal slap, with a claim you never gave, with a detailed list of everything that hurt you. And it's okay to feel that. Forgiveness does not begin from peace, but from wounding.

But eventually, if you want to truly heal, you'll have to go through that tricky terrain of forgiveness. And not for the other. For you. Because carrying resentment, guilt, repeated reproaches is like carrying a backpack full of emotional stones that don't let you move forward. And you're not here to crawl through the past. You're here to let go of it without it dragging you down.

Forgiving yourself is the first step

Sorry for having missed too much. For having shut you up. For having believed in excuses. For having lost yourself in the attempt to love. You weren't stupid. You were in love. You were learning. You were betting. You did the best you could with what you knew at the time. And now, you know more. Now, you choose yourself. So don't keep beating yourself up for not knowing earlier what you now understand with pain.

Forgiving Your Ex (If Possible and Healthy)

This is not about justifying what he did to you. It is not a matter of saying "it was not that serious" or smiling at him again out of emotional courtesy. Forgiving your ex doesn't mean you should talk to them again, or keep friendship, or erase everything that hurt. It means to stop wishing him punishment. Stop repeating their mistakes in your head. Stop giving it space in your peace of mind.

And if you can't forgive yet, don't force yourself. Not all waivers arrive on time. Sometimes, true forgiveness happens when you're not even thinking about it anymore. But the important thing is that you don't get caught up in hate, because hatred also binds. It also links. It also robs you of energy.

To forgive is to let go of the illusion that the past can change. It is to accept that what was, was. That you are no longer there. That you can look back without getting stuck. And that you can move forward lighter, without carrying around what you can't fix.

It is not easy. It's not fast. But it is liberating. And it is not done for the other. It's done for you. So that your story does not get stuck in a chapter of pain. So that, when you close this book, you don't close it with anger, but calmly. Strongly. With dignity. And with enough forgiveness so that you don't want to repeat what you don't want to live again.

Breaking the Cycle: How to Avoid Repeating the Same Mistakes

Getting out of a relationship hurts, but repeating the same story under a different name hurts more. Because there's nothing more frustrating than thinking "this time will be different"... and find yourself in the same emotional loop, with the same wounds, the same broken promises, the same tears on new plates. Breaking the cycle is not luck, it is awareness. And yes, it costs. But it's the shortest path to a freer, healthier, more emotional life.

The first step: acknowledge your part with brutal honesty

It's not about blaming yourself but about looking at yourself without disguise. Where did you overdeliver? What signs did you ignore? What promises did you make to yourself and then break yourself? What pattern do you continue to attract: absent, dependent, unequal loves? The cycle is only broken when you take responsibility for your choices, without excuses and without romanticism.

Second: stop idealizing love as salvation

You are not incomplete. You don't need someone to come to "rescue" you, or a relationship that makes you feel valuable. As long as you keep looking for someone to fix you, you're going to keep falling into ties where you end up broken. Love is not an emotional band-aid, it is a complement to what you already are. And you're enough.

Third: Define your boundaries before you fall in love, not after

If you don't know what you're not going to tolerate, you'll end up tolerating it. Make a list of your non-negotiables and be clear about it before opening your heart again. Because when you have no defined limits, you become moldable to the desire of others. And that, sooner or later, devastates you.

Fourth: listen more to what you feel than to what you are told

Words make you fall in love, but actions reveal. He stops justifying inconsistencies with excuses such as "but sometimes he does show me that he cares about me". Sometimes it's not enough. The pattern repeats itself when you hear promises and silence your intuition. Next time, believe more in what makes you uncomfortable than what excites you.

Fifth: Don't confuse intensity with true love

The drama, the ups and downs, the jealousy disguised as passion... All of that can feel addictive, but it's not healthy love. It's an emotional roller coaster. And every time you go up without an emotional belt, you fall harder. Real love doesn't make you tremble with anxiety. It gives you peace.

And finally: make self-knowledge your compass

Do therapy if you can. Writes. Read. Talk to yourself honestly. Learn from you. Because the more you know yourself, the less you betray yourself. And when you don't betray yourself, you choose better. No longer from emotional hunger, but from fullness.

Breaking the cycle is not promising that you will never fail again. It's deciding that this time you're not going to ignore yourself. That you are no longer going to enter a relationship with the blindfold on. That you don't need to repeat the lesson to learn it. Because this time, it's no longer about finding the love of your life. It's about never getting lost again. And that, yes, is love. The good kind. The one that starts with you.

Idealized nostalgia vs. reality

One of the quietest enemies after a breakup isn't your ex... it's your selective memory. The one that erases all discussions, minimizes tears and turns any beautiful moment into an epic poem worthy of Netflix. Suddenly, you miss things that you didn't even like that much. You miss the routine, the good morning with emojis, the smell of his perfume, how he hugged you when you didn't even know why you were together. Sound familiar? That's not love. It is idealized nostalgia. And it is a trap.

Idealized nostalgia is like a poorly edited movie: only the best scenes stayed, with background music, perfect lighting, and meaningful silences. But if you rewind honestly, there are also chapters that hurt, dialogues that broke you, gestures that you ignored and emptiness that you filled by dint of hope. Don't be fooled: you miss him, yes... But not everything was as beautiful as your mind wants you to believe.

And no, you're not crazy. The brain does it for survival. Sometimes he clings to the good to justify what hurt. Because it hurts less to think that you lost something beautiful than to accept that you were in a place that was not healthy. But idealizing the past is the most direct way to relapse, to return, to repeat. Because he confuses "it was beautiful at times" with "it can still work".

So, how do you stop that nostalgia that embellishes what did you wrong? Remembering the concrete details. How did you feel about yourself when you were with that person? How many times did you go to bed with lumps in your throat? What things did you stop being, doing, saying to keep the peace? Make lists. Write down what hurt, what you kept silent, what you tolerated. Not to hate. To remember clearly.

It is not about erasing the beautiful moments. It is about ceasing to turn them into an excuse to return to what no longer belongs to you. Sometimes love existed, yes... but it was not enough. Sometimes it was real, but it wasn't fair. Sometimes you gave it your all and that wasn't enough. And that is also part of the reality. Accepting it does not mean ceasing to feel. It means to stop lying to you.

Idealized nostalgia is comfortable, but it doesn't let you move forward. Reality, on the other hand, sometimes hurts... but it liberates. And only from that truth can you begin to write something new. Something more than yours. Something you don't have to embellish to endure. Because this time, it's not about remembering the good. It's about building something you don't have to forget.

Fear of loneliness, social pressure

One of the biggest monsters that appear after a breakup does not have the face of an ex, but of emptiness. It's that fear of loneliness that creeps into the house when you turn off the lights, when there are no more goodnight messages, when no one asks you how your day was. And to that fear is added another annoying voice: that of social pressure, which not only gives its opinion, but whispers things like "you should be with someone else now" or "and when do you?".

The fear of being alone is not weakness, it is human. We have always been taught that love is a goal, a destiny, a medal. If you don't have a partner, you're incomplete. That singleness is a kind of uncomfortable waiting room. But it is not. Loneliness is not failure. It's space. It is fertile silence. It is the place where you can listen to yourself again after so much noise from others.

Being alone does not mean being empty. It means being with you. And that, at first, can be dizzying, because we are not used to choosing ourselves without witnesses. But it is also there where you grow, where you recover parts of yourself that were diluted between appointments, sacrifices and concessions.

And what about social pressure? Let him wait. Let her give her own opinion. Let him stand in line. You're not here to fit into mold. You should not have a partner at a certain age, or get married to comply, or appear happy on social media with someone just to avoid uncomfortable questions at family gatherings. Your peace is worth more than any "what about your boyfriend?" Life is not a wedding race or a couple's photo parade. It is a path that is best traveled when you do not abandon yourself for fear of being unaccompanied.

You're alone now, yes. But you're not incomplete. You are with you. And when you learn to be with yourself without it hurting, without running to fill the space with anything, then you are ready to love again. Not out of necessity. By choice. And there, right there, the fear of loneliness no longer has power. Because you discovered that you don't need anyone to feel accompanied, as long as you don't leave yourself alone again. Never again.

The "comfort zone" of the known

Few things are as addictive as what you already know, even if it hurts. That's why so many people get back together with their exes, even if they know it's not convenient for them. That's why you find yourself reading old conversations, remembering only the good things, wondering if it really was that bad. The reason is not always love. Many times it is customary. False emotional security. The comfort zone where, even though you lacked something, you knew how to survive.

That area is treacherous. Not because it's comfortable, but because it's familiar. And the familiar, no matter how toxic, can feel safer than the new. Your mind prefers the known, even if it drags you into the same pain. Because you have already learned to walk with wounds. What you don't know is how to walk without them. And that's scary.

Getting out of there is like letting go of a rope without knowing if there is a net underneath. It is feeling that you are alone, unprotected, without reference. But you know what? That rope didn't hold you up. It tied you up. It kept you spinning at the same point, calling what was often disguised anxiety "love."

The comfort zone is that place where you repeated to yourself "it's not so bad" while your self-esteem melted in silence. Where you juggled emotionally to justify what had no justification. Where you were half you, half fear of change.

And yes, getting out of there is uncomfortable. You will feel nostalgia, doubts, temptations to return. But if you stand your ground, one day you realize that what seemed like security was resignation. What you call love is need. And that outside that area there is life. There are new versions of you that you don't know because you never let them breathe.

Stepping out of your comfort zone doesn't mean you're going to be okay right away. It means that you choose yourself, even if it hurts. That you bet on the unknown in the hope that, this time, you won't have to shrink to fit in.

Because when you let go of the known that hurts you, you make room for the unknown that can heal you. And that's where true freedom begins when you choose the risk of growing over the fear of repeating. Because you deserve more than to survive. You deserve to discover what is outside the circle that no longer has you.

Your Ex's Attempts to Get Back (and How to Handle Them)

It seems like a universal law: just when you start to breathe better, when you stop checking their profile, when you finally manage to sleep without checking your cell phone... Appears. Your ex. As if it had been invoked by your progress. Sometimes with a cryptic message like "how are you?", other times with an absurd excuse such as "I remembered you because I found your charger", and in the most blatant cases, with a statement worthy of a soap opera: "I realized that I love you". Aha.

Just because your ex wants to come back doesn't mean they should. A relapse is not a divine sign. It's just that: a relapse. And your job is not to analyze whether this time it is real. Your job is to ask yourself if this time you are willing to go back to the same place that hurt you.

First: Stop and breathe

Don't respond in the heat. Don't get your hopes up cold. Do your sanity a favor: save the message, take a step back, and ask yourself if what you feel is love... or addiction to the known. Sometimes you don't miss the person, but the routine, the validation, the role you had next to someone.

Second: remember why it ended

Remember, not from melancholy, but from clarity. What made you cry? What parts of you were turned off while there? How much did it cost you to leave? Rereading conversations, reviewing diaries, talking to a friend who lived the process with you can bring you back into focus. Healthy love does not leave carelessly or appear only when it loses you.

Third: Evaluate their intentions, not their words

Does he come back because he loves you or because he can't stand to see you move forward? Does he come back when he sees you strong or when he knows you're vulnerable? Does it return with new facts or with the same recycled promises? A "I have changed" without proof is worth nothing. Real repentance is seen, not said.

Fourth: Decide firmly, not nostalgically

If you decide not to open the door, let it be for you. Not out of anger. Not out of pride. For peace. For dignity. Because you deserve a love that doesn't have to lose you to value you. If you decide to listen, do it from your current version, not from the one you were still expecting crumbs.

And if you blocked it and it still insists, remember insisting is not love. It's ego. And love that returns impulse does not usually remain with commitment. So protect everything: your process, your peace, your new life.

Because this time you are not here to repeat. You have to choose for yourself. Even if your hand trembles. Even if it hurts. Even if part of you wants to say "yes." Choose your evolution. Not your past. Your ex has already had his chance. Now you have it. With you. Forever.

Reminders of why the relationship ended

When the heart begins to heal, but the mind becomes nostalgic, the famous "maybe it wasn't so bad", "I must have exaggerated", or the classic "maybe we'll change both and this time it will work" appear. No. High. Breathe. That's not the universe giving you a sign, it's your memory cheating you. And because of that, you need clear, head-to-head, no-sugar-added reminders of why that relationship ended. Because if not, you run the risk of romanticizing your own wound.

1. You felt lonely even when you were accompanied

A partner who is not emotionally present is not company, it is an empty mirror. You were there, but you felt ignored, not heard, not seen. And that, over time, broke you more than any argument.

2. You wore yourself out trying to save something that wasn't yours alone

You did your part. Too many. You justified, you forgave, you gave opportunities that were not earned. But a relationship is not built on patches, sacrifices and unilateral hopes. It's not love if only you pushed the boat.

3. You annulled yourself to bother us

You kept quiet about what hurt you. You adapted. You gave in. You became the least free version of yourself to keep the peace. And that "love" that demanded that you stop being you was not love. It was control, fear or dependence.

4. You weren't valued as you deserved

Perhaps there were subtle slights. Constant criticism. Indifference. Or simply a lack of reciprocity that left you emotionally empty. The love that doesn't take care of you, that doesn't respect you, that doesn't celebrate you... it is not love, no matter how many kisses there have been.

5. They broke your trust (and the scar still burns)

A betrayal, a lie, an infidelity, or many small disappointments that made you live on alert. You were in "emotional detective" mode all the time. And a relationship that needs surveillance is not a home. It is a cold war.

6. You weren't happy, even though you repeated it to yourself as a mantra

You tried to convince yourself that it was normal to feel that way. That all couples go through this. Maybe the problem was you. But your body doesn't lie. Your sleepless nights, your tears, your constant doubts... That was your intuition screaming.

7. Dating costs you so much, that going back would be betraying you

Don't forget how much it hurt to leave. How much you fought against yourself not to return. How much it cost you to rebuild your routine, your self-esteem, your identity? Going back is not romantic. It's breaking yourself again with your eyes open.

These reminders are not to be hated, nor to live with grudges. They're to keep you ground. So that you do not return to what has already shown you that it was not your place. Because whenever your heart softens with sweet memories, these motifs will be there to remind you of the full truth. And the truth is clear: you came out because you deserved more. And you still deserve it. Don't forget. Never again.

Having an "escape plan" for times of weakness

Because yes, it is going to happen. There will be a gray day, a sleepless night, a treacherous song, or simply a gust of loneliness that hits your chest with the desire to write "hello, how are you?". And in that instant, your emotional brain is going to look for excuses ("I just want to know if it's okay"), your ego is going to want to check if it misses you, and your wound is going to scream that maybe, just maybe, you should come back. That's why you need an escape plan before weakness catches you unprepared.

1. Your "emotional emergency box"

Literally or symbolically, have a list with reminders of why you came out: phrases, diary entries, power songs or that photo where you didn't even recognize yourself from so much pain. Your present self has to protect your future self when it falters. Leave clues so you don't get lost.

2. Create a list of concrete actions

– Call that friend who won't let you relapse

– Go for a walk without a cell phone

– Go take a shower as if it were a purification ritual

– Reread this book or this chapter

– Put on a movie where the protagonist doesn't get back together with his ex

In moments of weakness, the brain needs structure, not deep reflections.

3. Preventive blocking: no access, no relapse

If you know that watching it online tempts you, if you know that a story destabilizes you... Mute, cut, block. Not to punish him. To protect you. And if you unlocked it "just out of curiosity," lock again without drama. Your peace is worth more than that doubt.

4. Have short sentences that cut off relapse

Write a phrase like "if I come back, I'll get lost again" or "I already promised myself not to beg for affection" and stick it on your mirror, on the wallpaper, on the door of the fridge. In moments of impulsivity, a clear phrase can be an anchor.

5. Make a pact with yourself

Promise yourself that before you write to him or relapse, you're going to do at least three things on your list. If after that you still want to come back...

Ok, but do the whole process. Nine out of ten, you won't want to.

6. Remember: It's an emotion, not an order

Having a slump doesn't mean you should take action. The desire to return is like an emotional craving: if you let it go, it goes down. You don't need to "figure it out" on the spot. Just breathe, resist, and let the impulse not rule you.

Having a plan doesn't make you weak. It makes you wise. Because it's not about feeling, but about not letting a temporary emotion destroy everything you've built. Your peace is not negotiated on a night of nostalgia. Prepare for vulnerable moments... Because that's also part of loving you.

Visualize your future without your ex

Closing a cycle does not only imply letting go of the past, it is also about opening space to imagine what is coming. And when you're getting out of a relationship, that sounds impossible. Your mind keeps revolving around what was, what could have been, and what will no longer be. Visualizing the future without your ex isn't easy, but it's essential. It's that moment when you stop surviving... to create.

And no, it's not about imagining yourself dancing alone on the beach in a white dress while everything slips you down. It's about visualizing a version of you that is no longer defined by that story. A woman who does not carry sadness as a backpack or fear as a compass. A woman who doesn't need to have a partner to feel complete, and who no longer asks herself "what would he think of this?", but "does this do me good?"

Visualizing your future is building new references. Imagine waking up in peace, without checking your cell phone. Laughing out loud with new friends. Studying that which you always postponed. Traveling alone or with someone who does add to you. Living in a space of yours, decorated with everything you like and with no one to criticize it. Doing things that you didn't do before because he wasn't interested in them.

Maybe you visualize yourself strongly, leading a project. Or quietly, cultivating your garden. Or free, by boarding a plane with a one-way ticket. The how doesn't matter so much. The important thing is that you're not waiting for anyone to get started.

And if you have a hard time imagining that future, start with small fragments: a day without anxiety, a meal you cook for yourself, a night where you fall asleep without tears. The future does not arrive as a movie. It comes in new scenes that you decide to write.

When you visualize your life without your ex, you're not erasing him: you're leaving him in his rightful place. Part of your history, not the center of your existence. And in doing so, you open the door to what's most important: you. No filters. Fearless. Without repeating what no longer belongs to you.

The future is not what "comes". The future is what you are building today with every decision, every boundary, every act of self-love. And that future, even if you don't see it clearly yet, no longer needs its shadow to shine. Because this time, the sun rises for you. Just for you.

Digital Detox: Unfollow, Mute, Archive

Today, a breakup does not end when you say "goodbye". It ends when you do digital cleaning. Because no matter how much you block emotionally, if you keep seeing your ex smiling on Instagram uploading suspiciously indirect phrases, or changing your look as if you had graduated from the "look how good I am without you" course ... Your mind never stops letting go. And your heart, less so.

Digital detox is not drama, it is self-care. It's not about being radical, it's about being realistic: you can't heal if you keep spying on the wound every day.

1. Unfollowing is not immature. It's smart.

If every time you go on Instagram you feel a pang because you saw that they liked someone or uploaded a photo of a "new stage", what are you gaining? Nothing. Only anxiety. Unfollowing your ex, their friends, their family, or any emotional satellites around them is not revenge. It's mental hygiene.

2. Mute: the intermediate step for the brave in process

If you're not ready to cut it yet, mute. Stories, posts, notifications. Out of your sight, out of the loop. You don't need to see everything he does to confirm that he's still alive. You no longer need to be in that emotional cinema where you repeat the same movie with a sad ending.

3. Archive: Clean without cutting if you still can't let go

Photos, messages, memories. If you're not ready to cut, archive. It takes out of visual scope everything that traps you in nostalgia. You don't have to destroy everything, but you do have to move it out of the danger zone. Because a bad day + an old photo = relapse assured.

4. Stop surveillance with real rules

Set boundaries with yourself: "I'm not going to review his profile for seven days", "if I go in, I have to write down what I feel afterwards". And if you fall... Don't beat yourself up. But don't justify yourself either. Take note of the emotional downturn that doing so left you with. That is the best motivation not to repeat it.

5. Do extended emotional cleansing

Delete conversations that no longer make sense. Get out of groups where it's still mentioned. Delete the songs that drag you down. Create a digital space where you are the center, not your past.

A true digital detox isn't about him. It's about you. About stopping opening windows that no longer lead anywhere. About turning off external noise so I can hear you. And, above all, about choosing you every time nostalgia knocks on the door disguised as "I just wanted to see what he's doing".

Your peace is worth more than a glance. Your progress, more than a story. And your dignity... you don't negotiate with the algorithm.

What to do with objects and memories

There comes that moment in the love duel in which you come across the sweater he lent you, the letter he wrote to you, the happy photos framed as if everything had been perfect... And you feel like the past jumps at you like it never went away. What to do with all that? Throw? Save? Burn it in a cathartic campfire to the rhythm of a song of spite? Spoiler: it depends. But what is clear is that acting as if nothing is there does not work. It's time to face it.

1. Do an emotional review, not just a visual one

Look at each object and ask yourself: does this remind me of a happy version of me or an open wound? Not everything that comes from the past deserves to stay. Some memories are of the anchors. Others, mirrors. And others... garbage in the shape of nostalgia.

2. Create a transition box

If you're not ready to let go completely, store everything in a box. Call it what you want: "Cassi's Grave box," whatever. The important thing is that these objects are not plain in sight, decorating your room like ghosts with good taste. Store them in a hard-to-reach place. If in six months you didn't even miss them... you know what to do.

3. Give away, donate or recycle what does not have emotional weight

T-shirts, impersonal gifts, books that were never really yours. If they don't break you, they don't tie you up. Take them out of your physical space to start clearing your emotional space as well. Because the place occupied by "what was" is the same one that "what may come" could be using.

4. Burn, break, or cut if you need to (yes, really)

If there are letters that hurt you, photos that make you relapse, objects that symbolize broken promises... Do a ritual. You don't have to set fire to the drama Queen (although it sounds tempting). But you can write a final letter, break what hurts, close the cycle with a physical action. Sometimes the body needs a gesture for the soul to understand that it is over.

5. Digital: photos, messages, also count

Clean up your gallery, networks, and files. Erase what you know makes your stomach turn. If you can't yet, create a hidden folder. But set a review date: your healing can't depend on a collection of selfies with filters and expired promises.

6. Whatever you decide to keep, let it be out of self-love, not attachment

If there's something you really value, that doesn't hurt you, and that is part of your personal story beyond the relationship, keep it with respect. But don't let it stop you from moving forward, or make you go backwards every time you see it. The memory can stay... as long as it doesn't catch you.

Your space reflects your process. And if you want to move forward, you need what surrounds you to sustain you, not sabotage you. You're not throwing things away. You're shedding weight. You are making room for the new. You are saying to the universe, and to yourself: I don't forget what I have experienced, but I am no longer trapped there. And that... it is liberation.

The difference between loneliness and being alone

They look the same, but they're not. Being alone is a circumstance. Feeling lonely is an emotional state. One is external, the other is internal. You can be surrounded by people and feel alone or be completely alone and feel at peace. And after a breakup, that difference becomes crucial. Because you're not running away from loneliness... You're running away from the emptiness that comes when you disconnect from yourself.

To be alone is to be without physical company at a certain time. You can choose to have dinner with yourself, spend a weekend with no plans or sleep in a bed that now has more space. It is literal. It is neutral. And sometimes, it is even necessary. It is the space where your inner voice stops competing with the noise of others.

Loneliness, on the other hand, is emotional. It is that feeling of being abandoned, forgotten, misunderstood. It doesn't always show up when you're alone. Sometimes it comes up in the middle of a relationship where you are not heard, at a party where you pretend to be fine, or even in a conversation where you laugh while inside you break down. Loneliness is the absence of connection: with yourself, with others, with something that makes sense to you.

After a breakup, we confuse the two all the time. We are afraid of being alone because we believe that this is the same as feeling empty. But no. What hurts is not being without that person, it is not knowing what to do with the silence they left. The problem is not free time, it is the lack of purpose, emotional companionship, internal structure.

The good news is that being alone can become your safe place if you learn to inhabit it without running away. It can become the space where you discover what you like without having to share it, where you laugh with yourself without justifying yourself, where you hold yourself without having to beg for attention.

Loneliness is not cured by external company. It is relieved with internal presence. And when you learn to be alone without feeling lonely, you stop accepting crumbs just because you have someone by your side. Because you are no longer afraid of silence. Because you no longer need someone to choose you to feel valuable.

Being alone is freedom. Solitude is the bridge you cross to meet yourself. And when you cross that bridge... There is no turning back. Because you realize that true love doesn't come when someone fills your emptiness, but when you stop fearing them. And that's where everything new begins.

Emotional independence as a superpower

For years we were led to believe that true love was needing each other. That if you didn't suffer for someone, it wasn't intense. Which, if it didn't hurt, wasn't deep. That being "whole" was only possible next to another. But the truth is that emotional independence not only does not ruin love... it makes it more real, healthier, and much more powerful. Because when you stop needing someone to feel alive, free, or enough, you become your own source. And that, my dear, is a superpower.

Being emotionally independent doesn't mean you don't feel, don't love, or don't need affection. It means that you don't fall apart if you are not loved. That you can hold yourself when everything is moving. That you do not hand over your stability in the hands of anyone, no matter how much you are in love.

It's looking someone in the eye and saying: I love you, but I don't need you to be happy. It's choosing to stay out of desire, not out of fear of being alone. It's being able to hear a "no" without your world falling apart. It is having space for the other without losing your own.

When you are emotionally independent:

— You don't accept crumbs because you're no longer hungry for yourself.

- Don't keep quiet about your needs for fear of abandonment.

— You don't emotionally juggle someone to stay.

— You don't beg for affection, or chase answers, or seek closure where there is only silence.

Having this superpower doesn't make you a cold, inaccessible rock. It turns you into a woman who no longer negotiates her peace. In someone who loves freedom, not from lack. In someone who can be alone without feeling empty... and went without ceasing to be her.

The best part? That you don't need to be born with this power. It is cultivated. Day by day. Decision by decision. Limit to limit. It is the result of healing, of knowing yourself, of falling and getting up without waiting for someone to come to your rescue.

And when you have it, something changes you attract more authentic, more balanced, more honest bonds. Because when you no longer abandon yourself, no one else can do it without you noticing.

Emotional independence is not a shield against love. It is the foundation for better love. Because when you don't need anyone to breathe anymore... Then yes, you're ready to fly. On your axis. In your center. In your possession. And this time, you don't fall. You rise.

When do you know you're ready to go out again?

There is no exact date, no magic formula, no alarm that sounds one day and says: "congratulations, you are over your ex, go out and fall in love again". Knowing if you're ready to go out again doesn't depend on the calendar... it's up to you. And it's not measured by how many weeks passed, but by how you feel when you're no longer running away from the past or looking for an emotional patch.

You're ready when you choose first. When you no longer look to distract yourself from emptiness, but to share from fullness. When you no longer idealize anyone who smiles at you. When you don't confuse attention with connection, you don't cling to the first person who writes to you just because silence makes you less uncomfortable with notifications turned on.

You're ready when seeing your ex doesn't move you anymore. Not because you hate it or because you don't care, but because it no longer occupies the center of your narrative. Because you no longer compare it to every new person you meet. Because you don't feel the urge to prove that "I can rebuild my life too" as if it were an emotional competition from Instagram.

You're ready when you know yourself better. When you know what you want, what you are not going to tolerate, what you need in a relationship and what mistakes you do not intend to repeat. When your limits are no longer sandcastles that unravel with any wave of attention.

You are also ready when you can be alone and feel peace, not heartache. When dating is a choice and not a necessity. Because the healthiest love doesn't come when you're desperate for someone to rescue you, but when you've already discovered that you don't need anyone to save you.

And if you ask yourself: but am I afraid to open up again, that's normal. Fear is not a sign that you are not ready. It's a sign that you've learned. The important thing is where you decide from: from the wound or from the healing? From hunger or from desire?

So don't rush. Don't skip your own rhythm due to external pressure or poorly managed loneliness. When the time comes, you'll know. It will feel different. Quieter. More honest. More you. And this time, you're going to enter into love not to complete yourself... but to share with you. Whole. Conscious. Free. And without fear of starting over.

Avoid "rebound" relationships

Just as you come out of a breakup, with your heart half-scared and self-esteem faltering, someone new appears. He smiles at you nicely, listens to you, responds quickly to your messages, and suddenly you feel butterflies... or at least a little relief. And that's when the famous "bounce" comes into the picture. That relationship that is not really a new beginning, but an emotional extension of what you have not yet closed.

Rebound relationships often seem intense, urgent, even magical. But they are not born of the authentic desire to connect. They are born from the fear of emptiness. Of the desire to show that you have already overcome everything, even if inside you are still looking back. And if you're not attentive, what seems like an opportunity ends up becoming another emotional grief that you didn't even know you were going to have to process.

How do you know if you're entering a rebound relationship?

— If it gives you peace because it distracts you, not because it nourishes you

— If you're more focused on forgetting your ex than getting to know the new person

— If you're adjusting too quickly without really knowing how you're feeling

— If you fear being alone rather than getting excited about what is being born

— If you idealize the bond with phrases like "this is just what I needed after so much pain" (surprise: it probably isn't)

The problem with rebound relationships isn't the new person. It's that you're still emotionally in another story. And using someone to fill a void that only you can close is an unintentional way to harm you... and the other.

So what to do?

- Breathe. Not every romantic interest needs to be explored right away.

— Give yourself permission to meet people without it implying a match.

— Be honest with yourself: are you looking for affection or validation?

— Remember that healing is not a race. And being alone for a while is not punishment, it is preparation.

Avoiding a rebound relationship does not mean closing yourself off to love. It means giving yourself the respect of not starting something new while you're still patched up inside. It means telling you: I deserve to enter my next story from clarity, not from pain. And that choice, even if no one sees it... it is self-love in its most elegant form.

Communication and limits in new relationships

When you decide to open your heart again, after a breakup that taught you more than you wanted to learn, it's easy to fall into two extremes: closing yourself completely so as not to get hurt again... or throwing yourself with everything as if the past had left no marks. But if you really want to build something new and healthy, you need two things: clear communication and firm boundaries. Not to protect you from love, but to protect your peace within love.

Communication is not talking a lot, it is speaking truthfully

From the beginning, be you. Not the version that pleases, not the one that "doesn't want to seem intense", not the one that adapts quickly for fear of losing. He speaks from the center, not from fear. Say what you expect, what is good for you, what you are not willing to repeat. You don't need to recount your full trauma on the first date, but you can say, "I value honesty," "I don't look for games," "I take bonds seriously." Clarity scares away those who do not come with good intentions. And bless him.

Limits do not distance, they filter

A boundary is not a wall, it is a lockable door. Whoever knows how to play, enters. Whoever does not respect, is left out. Your boundaries should be defined before you fall in love, because once the heart is engaged, tolerance masquerades as understanding. Put your non-negotiables on the table without fear of sounding tough. The right people are not scared of your limits, they are grateful for them.

Examples of healthy and necessary limits:

"If you disappear without warning, that's not for me."

– "It doesn't suit me to talk every day if there is no clear link."

"I don't want a relationship where I have to guess how you feel."

– "I don't tolerate disrespect, not even in jest."

And remember silence also communicates

If he doesn't listen to you, if he minimizes your emotions, if he makes fun of your limits, if he avoids having uncomfortable conversations... That also says a lot. Do not explain more than necessary to those who have no real interest in understanding you. Your energy is worth more than a repeated explanation.

Your new relationship doesn't have to be perfect, but it does have to be healthy

And for that, you need to have the courage to speak up from the beginning. Not to control the other, but to build something together from authenticity. With space, with respect, with clarity.

Communication connects you. Boundaries protect you. And both, combined, allow you to love without getting lost in the attempt. This time, it's different. This time, with awareness. This time, with you in the center. As it should always have been.

The importance of compatibility and shared values

When the heart is in love, the mind usually goes into "anything can be done" mode. And of course, at first, everything seems to work: conversations flow, there is chemistry, they laugh at the same nonsense... But over time, what really sustains a relationship is not whether they like the same series, but whether they share values, goals, and ways of seeing life.

The compatibility is not that they like the same types of pizza. It is that they have similar rhythms, similar expectations, healthy ways of resolving conflicts, similar ideas about what it means to love, to care, to be committed. It's being able to build something without having to leave essential parts of yourself along the way.

Shared values are those invisible pillars that support the relationship when falling in love becomes a daily occurrence. They are the deep beliefs: respect, honesty, fidelity, freedom, commitment, family, spirituality, work, money, personal growth. They do not have to think the same about everything, but they do have to think about the essentials. Because if you dream of building a life as a couple based on respect and communication, and the other person sees love as something casual and without emotional responsibility... Guess who's going to end up with a pureed heart.

Emotional compatibility matters, too. If you are expressive and the other person avoids talking about what they feel; if you believe in growing up together and he runs away when something gets serious; if you value brutal honesty and he hides behind passive-aggressive silences... There is no middle ground: there is wear and tear.

And it's not about changing the other or adapting yourself. It's about finding someone you are with without having to explain the obvious. Where you don't have to negotiate your values to fit in or justify your needs so as not to seem "difficult".

Because when there is real compatibility, love is not about constant sacrifice. It's about cooperation, fluidity, being aligned on what's important. Differences can add up, but only if the foundations are strong and shared.

Don't ignore the signs with the excuse of passion. Chemistry ignites, but values sustain. And if you're not walking in the same direction, it doesn't matter how much attraction there is... sooner or later you're going to get tired of paddling alone.

So this time, before you jump into the void of "maybe it will work", ask yourself: do we have what it takes to build? Or just what is needed to entertain us for a while? Because you are no longer for relationships with an end date. You are to build love with roots. And that begins by choosing consciously, not urgently.

Lessons learned and wisdom gained

Every breakup, no matter how heartbreaking, comes with a gift disguised as catastrophe: the possibility of learning. Of course, at first all you want is for it to stop hurting, for the world to give you back your dignity and for the pillow not to smell of defeat. But over time, when the emotional dust settles, something is activated: a new lucidity, a kind of radar that you didn't have before. We call it wisdom. We call it evolution. We call it: "now I know what I don't want or go crazy."

A failed relationship doesn't define you. But it does reveal you. It shows you your blind spots, your hidden needs, your emptiness disguised as romanticism. And if you dare to look honestly, you will discover that that "mistake" was, in fact, a teacher with cold hands and a direct voice.

Lessons that many of us learn with emotional blood but that are worth gold:

— Loving does not mean losing yourself.

— Prolonged silence is also a response.

- If you have to beg for attention, it's not love.

— Jealousy is not passion, it is insecurity with perfume.

— What begins with anxiety rarely ends in peace.

— Love doesn't hurt what hurts is the absence of self-love.

Post-breakup wisdom isn't about turning cold or shutting down love. On the contrary: it is a matter of choosing better, of recognizing signs earlier, of taking care of yourself with more tenderness, of loving with more awareness and less blind illusion.

Now you know that you don't need to get lost in anyone to feel accompanied. Being alone is not a curse, but an opportunity. That next time you are not going to romanticize intensity, but value stability. That you are not interested in repeating history under another name, but in writing a new one with another pen: your own.

And if you're wondering if it was worth so much pain to get here, think about this: you're now a stronger, more lucid, more whole version of yourself. Now you no longer confuse attachment with love, attention with affection, promises with deeds. Now you no longer fall in love with potential, but with realities. And that... it is the real closure.

You didn't come out broken. You came out awakened.

And that is, perhaps, the greatest victory.

Your resilience and strength

You may not notice it yet, but you're here. Reading this. Breathing. Advancing. Even if sometimes you drag your feet, even if it hurts, even if you don't understand how you got to this point. And that, even if you don't see it on social media or have medals, is a form of courage. Because there is something profoundly powerful about moving forward when everything inside you asks you to surrender. That's called resilience. And you have it.

Resilience is not "being strong" all the time. It's not swallowing tears, or smiling while pretending, or convincing the world that you're okay. Resilience is allowing you to fall without staying on the ground. It's having uncomfortable conversations with yourself. It is to rebuild yourself from the pieces, without a manual, without guarantees, only with the stubborn desire to feel peace again.

Your strength is not measured by how much you have let go, but by how much you have learned to let go. For every "no" you had a hard time saying. For every message you didn't send, even though you were dying to do so. For every time you choose yourself, trembling, instead of going back to the same familiar cycle just for fear of being alone.

And no, it wasn't easy. It's not. But here you are. With a scarred heart, yes, but also with a new lucidity, a renewed dignity, and an emotional compass that you didn't have before. You built all of that. At your own pace. In your own way. With every uncomfortable decision you make for your well-being.

Your resilience is not invincible, nor does it need to be. It is okay to cry, to falter, to retreat. The important thing is that you haven't given up completely. Even on grey days, you should continue to bet on yourself. That you continue to believe – even if it's just a little bit – that the best is yet to come.

Because the truth is that you are not the same as before. You're wiser. More careful. More compassionate with you. And that strength that you carry inside you today, that which is not always noticeable on the outside, is what will sustain you in the next chapter. One that you are going to write from your center, not from your wound.

So look at yourself with respect. Not because of what you lost, but because of everything you survived. And remember: if you were able to get out of there, you will be able to get where you want to go. Because your strength no longer screams. Walk with you. Firm. Serena. And ready to start again, this time... with you in charge.

You're stronger than you think

Summary of the key points

Surviving a breakup isn't just letting someone go, it's finding yourself again. Sometimes it seems impossible, other times it hurts more than you thought you could bear. But step by step, tear after tear, silence after silence, something begins to heal. And if you've made it this far, if you've gone through this entire reading, if you're doing the work of looking inward, then let me remind you in all its letters: you're stronger than you think.

Let's review what you have already sown in this process:

— You acknowledged the pain without minimizing or disguising it. You understood that there are no shortcuts, and that grief is a necessary part of the journey.

— You learned to feel your emotions without fear, confirming your sadness, your anger, your confusion, and giving them space without letting them define you.

— You discovered what zero contact is, how to implement it, and why it is vital to rebuild yourself away from emotional relapses.

— You began to reconnect with yourself, with your values, your passions, your goals, your autonomy, your health and your overall well-being.

— You understood that healthy love is not born from a vacuum, and that you don't need a rebound or external validation to feel valuable.

— You reminded yourself that being alone is not the same as being empty, and that solitude can be fertile ground to flourish.

— You began to practice conscious communication and firm limits in your new relationships, not from fear, but from self-respect.

— You learned to find patterns, to forgive from the heart (and not from naivety), and to choose again without repeating what has already broken you.

— You reaffirmed that emotional compatibility and shared values are more important than any momentary butterfly.

— And, above all, you understood that your resilience is not measured by how much love you gave, but by how much love you gave back to yourself.

Every step you took was a seed. And even if you only see disturbed earth now, over time you will see a firmer, more conscious, more luminous version of you sprout. You are no longer looking for someone to save you. You no longer pursue love as if you are not worthy to receive it without pain. Now you walk with a new certainty: if you have me, I am no longer lost.

This is not the end. It is rebirth.

And you, brave soul, are doing better than you think.

Remember: It's not about surviving your ex, it's about surviving yourself when you loved someone who didn't love you well.

About The Author

Alina A. Rubi is a psychologist, writer and trainer who is passionate about the power of words and listening to transform lives. Over the years, she has dedicated her career to going with people in their processes of self-knowledge, emotional healing and personal development, always from a warm, respectful and deeply human perspective.

Graduated in Psychology, Alina specialized in working with family ties, interpersonal dynamics and patterns learned from childhood. Its integrative approach combines sound theory with a close, empathetic look at each person's unique experiences. She has worked in both individual consultation and workshops and group spaces, helping others understand the root of their emotional wounds, build healthy boundaries and redefine the way they relate to themselves and others.

Alina firmly believes that psychology is not just a field of study, but a bridge to personal freedom. That is why she dedicates a good part of her time to writing, convinced that psychological knowledge should be available to everyone. Her accessible and thoughtful texts look to offer clarity on often taboo topics such as family trauma, guilt, difficulty in saying "no" or the weight of invisible loyalties. His style combines professional rigor with simple and often humorous language, to help digest truths that may be uncomfortable but necessary.

In addition to her clinical practice and her facet as a writer, Alina has also taken part in training programs for professionals and has collaborated in community projects focused on mental health. He is especially interested in prevention: teaching us to recognize harmful patterns before they are perpetuated from generation to generation. For her, breaking family cycles is not an act of betrayal, but the greatest possible sign of love: the conscious decision not to inherit the same pain to others.

A faithful defender of the power of listening, Alina believes that many wounds begin where no one could, or wanted, to truly listen. That is why in his consultation he gives room to all voices: even to the most hurt, angry or embarrassed parts of each person. Its aim is that each one can reconcile with their history, signify it and live with more authenticity and peace.

Today, Alina Rubi continues to write, attend, teach and learn. Her work is a testament to her deep conviction: that we all deserve to build a life in which we don't have to choose between loving others and respecting ourselves. Because for her, psychology is much more than a profession: it is a tool for each person to become the conscious and compassionate narrator of their own story.

www.ingramcontent.com/pod-product-compliance
Lightning Source LLC
LaVergne TN
LVHW090413210926
848480LV00002B/549
* 9 7 9 8 2 3 1 4 1 6 9 4 3 *